# More ot
## The World's Best
## Drinking Jokes

*In this series:*

The World's Best Acting Jokes
The World's Best After-Dinner Jokes
The World's Best Boss Jokes
The World's Best Business Jokes
The World's Best Cricket Jokes
The World's Best Dirty Jokes
More of the World's Best Dirty Jokes
The World's Best Dirty Limericks
The World's Best Dirty Songs
The World's Best Dirty Stories
The World's Best Doctor Jokes
The World's Best Drinking Jokes
The World's Best Fishing Jokes
The World's Best Football Jokes
The World's Best Gardening Jokes
The World's Best Golf Jokes
More of the World's Best Golf Jokes
The World's Best Holiday Jokes
The World's Best Irish Jokes
More of the World's Best Irish Jokes
Still More of the World's Best Irish Jokes
The World's Best Jewish Jokes
More of the World's Best Jewish Jokes
The World's Best Lawyer Jokes
The World's Best Light-bulb Jokes
The World's Best Marriage Jokes
The World's Best Mother-in-law Jokes
The World's Best Motoring Jokes
The World's Best Scottish Jokes
The World's Best Skiing Jokes

# More of
# the World's
# Best
# Drinking Jokes

## Edward Phillips

### Illustrations by
### Andy Hunt

HarperCollins*Publishers*

HarperCollins*Publishers*
77–85 Fulham Palace Road,
Hammersmith, London W6 8JB

This paperback edition 1995
3  5  7  9  8  6  4  2

First published in Great Britain by
HarperCollins*Publishers* 1993

Text copyright © Edward Phillips 1993
Illustrations copyright © Andy Hunt 1993

The Author asserts the moral right to
be identified as the author of this work

ISBN 0 00 637959 1

Set in Goudy

Printed in Great Britain by
HarperCollinsManufacturing Glasgow

A wife decided she would leave her drunken husband, but a neighbour persuaded her to give him one more chance. 'Instead of nagging him,' she was advised, 'treat him nicely. Maybe he'll feel so ashamed, he'll stop drinking so heavily.' So the next night when he staggered home, she did not rant as usual. She made him a cup of tea, warmed his slippers, loosened his collar and tie and stroked his head. 'Shall we go to bed now?' she suggested.

'Might as well,' he replied. 'If I go home, there'll only be a row.'

Did you hear the one about the two drunks who were riding a roller coaster? Finally one turned to the other and said, 'You know, I think we got on the wrong bus!'

A doctor, hoping to cure a man of his alcoholism, asked him, 'How did you come to get so completely intoxicated?'

'I got into bad company, doctor,' he said. 'You see, there were four of us. I had a bottle of whisky, and the other three were teetotallers.'

In the course of an interview, a British wine expert visiting a French vineyard was asked by a reporter, 'Which do you think is more important, sex or wine?'

The connoisseur thought it over, then cautiously enquired, 'Claret or Burgundy?'

The drunk was on his way home after an afternoon drinking session. He accidentally wandered into the zoo and found himself in front of a cage containing a hippopotamus. 'Don't look at me like that, dear,' he stammered. 'I can explain everything!'

I like the way they test whisky in Kentucky. They take a jug of the stuff and send a charge of electricity through it. If the whisky turns sour, it's no good. But if it chases the current back to the generator, then it's ready for sale.

If you're drinking, don't drive to work. In fact, if you're drinking, don't go to work at all – stay home and have a ball.

A little boy of about ten went into a bar and sat down at one of the tables, all by himself. The barmaid came over and he said, 'Bring me a double Scotch.'

'You're under age – do you want to get me into trouble?' the waitress said.

'We'll talk about that later – just bring me my double Scotch.'

# THE DRINKER'S GUIDE TO BAR SIGNS

PLEASE DON'T FLATTER THE BARTENDER.
HE'D RATHER NOT CHANGE HIS OPINION
OF YOU.

PLEASE DO NOT INSULT OUR BARTENDERS.
CUSTOMERS WE CAN GET.

IF YOU ARE DRINKING TO FORGET, PLEASE
PAY FOR YOUR DRINKS IN ADVANCE.

NOT RESPONSIBLE FOR PATRONS LEFT
OVER 30 DAYS.

EVERYTHING ON SALE AT THE BAR IS OF
THE VERY FINEST QUALITY. EVEN THE
WATER HAS BEEN PASSED BY THE
MANAGEMENT.

DON'T CRY IN YOUR BEER. IT'S WEAK
ENOUGH AS IT IS.

YOUR WIFE CAN ONLY GET SO MAD.
RELAX AND HAVE ANOTHER ONE.

---

## IF YOU WANT TO RESIGN FROM ALCOHOLICS ANONYMOUS, WHY NOT DO IT HERE?

Did you hear the one about the drunk who got in a taxi and said, 'Eight times around Regent's Park – and make it schnappy!' For forty-five minutes the taxi circled Regent's Park with the drunk bouncing around in the back seat. Going into the fourth lap he got very excited. He leaned forward, grabbed the driver by the shoulder and yelled, 'Faster, you fool, faster! Can't you shee I'm in a hurry!'

It was a woman who drove me to drink. I still feel bad about it. I never wrote and thanked her.

A drunk walked into a bar and said, 'Give me a gim and tomic.'

The barman said, 'You're drunk – get out!'

The drunk went out, walked right round the block, came back in again, walked up to the bar and said, 'Give me a gim and tomic.'

The barman said, 'You're drunk – get out!'

Again the drunk walked out, right round the block, back in again, up to the bar, and said, 'Give me a gim and tomic.'

Again the barman said, 'You're drunk – get out!'

And the drunk said, 'Just a minute! Do you own all the pubs in this town?'

A fellow was sitting in a bar one evening when he noticed another customer knocking back double Scotches. As fast as the bartender served him, he tossed down the whisky in one gulp. 'That's no way to treat good whisky,' said the first customer.

'I know,' said the man, 'but it's the only way I've been able to drink them since my accident.'

'What sort of accident was it?' asked the first chap.

'It was awful,' said the second. 'I knocked one over with my elbow!'


A chap went into a pub and said to the barman, 'Give me a pint of your strongest and most expensive lager.' When the barman served him, he drank the lager down, and then groaned, 'Oh, I shouldn't have had that with what I've got!'

The barman said, 'Why — what have you got?' And the fellow said, '10p!'


A fellow suffering from severe toothache finally plucked up enough courage to go to the dentist. But his courage deserted him as soon as he sat down in the dentist's chair. 'You'd better have a tot of whisky to calm your nerves,' said the dentist.

After the patient had drunk the whisky, the dentist said, 'How do you feel now?'

'I'm still nervous,' said the patient, so the dentist gave him another tot of whisky. This was followed by a third, then a fourth, then a fifth.

'Have you got your courage back yet?' asked the dentist.

'I'll say!' said the patient, squaring his shoulders. 'I'd like to see the man who'd dare touch my teeth now!'

Contrary to popular opinion, pouring black coffee into a drunk doesn't do any good at all. All that happens is that you end up with a wide-awake drunk.

*First Drunk*: Gimme a Horse's Neck!
*Second Drunk*: I'll have a Horse's Tail! No sense in killing two horses!

Did you hear the one about the fellow who walked into a pub with a pig under his arm? The barman said, 'Where did you get that?'

'I won it in a raffle,' said the pig.

The landlord of a pub near Hyde Park had a beautiful Golden Labrador and every evening he used to get the barman to take it for a walk in the park and a swim in the Serpentine. And every evening the barman brought the dog back, tired, happy and damp. One night a customer said, 'I've seen that dog before.'

'Well, he's in here every night,' the landlord said.

'No, I've seen him somewhere else. I saw him tied to a tree outside the pub down the road. A chap came out of the pub and threw a bucket of water over him.'

A woman was discussing her husband with a friend in the supermarket. 'If the cigarette machine wasn't just a couple of feet from the bar,' she said, 'he'd get no exercise at all!'

Breaking with custom, a woman decided to have a Scotch and soda as a nightcap. After drinking it, she went upstairs to kiss her small son goodnight. As she bent to kiss him, he said, 'Mummy! You're wearing Daddy's perfume!'

Two inebriates staggered out of a pub at closing time. One of them was in a far worse state than the other and his friend said, 'You're in no condition to walk. Why don't you take a bus home?'
  'It wouldn't be any use,' muttered his pal. 'The wife wouldn't let me keep it in the houshe!'

Did you hear about the young man who took a young lady home to his flat? He offered her a Scotch and sofa and she reclined.

A married couple attended a cocktail party. After a couple of hours, the husband said, 'Don't have any more to drink, Mabel – your face is getting blurred!'

*Teacher*: Jimmy, I want you to spell 'straight'.
*Jimmy*: S–T–R–A–I–G–H–T.
*Teacher*: Correct. Now what does it mean?
*Jimmy*: Without water.

'I'll tell you what the matter is with you,' said the judge to the drunk in the dock. 'Alcohol! It's alcohol and alcohol alone that is responsible for your present troubles.'

'Thank you, Judge, thank you,' said the drunk. 'Everybody else says it's my own fault.'

A drunk was standing on the corner of the street when a policeman came up. 'Shay, offisher, where'sh the corner?' he mumbled.

'You're standing on it,' said the policeman.

'No wonder I couldn't find it!' said the drunk.

'Was your wife angry when you came home drunk last night?'

'Not really. I was going to have those front teeth out anyway.'

Two friends were returning from a convivial evening at the local. 'Am I staggering at all?' asked one. 'If I am, the wife'll notice it and there'll be hell to pay. Hang on here a minute – I'll walk on ahead and you tell me if I'm walking straight.'

He walked on a few steps and his mate said, 'You're all right – but the chap with you is staggering about all over the place.'

A fellow in the King's Head was boasting to all and sundry about his capacity for drink. One of the other customers began to get a bit fed up and said, 'See that big silver ice bucket on the counter? I'll bet you fifty pounds that if I fill that up with beer, you can't drink it down in one go.' The boaster turned on his heel and walked out of the pub.

Five minutes later he was back again and he asked the barman to fill the bucket with beer. He emptied it in record time.

'All right, you win,' said the fellow who had made the bet. 'But where did you rush off to just now?'

'Well,' said the boaster, 'I'd never tried that before so I popped into the pub next door to have a practice.'

During the days of Prohibition, a traveller found himself in a small town in Arkansas. He asked a man in the street where he could get a drink. 'Well,' said the man, 'in this town, they only use whisky for snake bites. There's only one snake in town, and it's gittin' kinda late. You'd better hurry down and git in line before it gits exhausted.'

At a bar in Toronto, a drunk was muttering, 'It can't be done! It can't be done!'

'What can't be done?' asked the bartender.

'That can't,' said the drunk, pointing to a big sign which read: DRINK CANADA DRY.

At a local trade union committee meeting, one of the delegates was somewhat the worse for drink. When the meeting came to the question of appointing permanent and temporary officers, the drunk got up to speak. 'Sit down!' hissed his neighbour. 'You're too drunk! I'll bet you don't even know the difference between temporary and permanent!'

'Oh, yesh I do!' said the drunk. 'I'm intoxicated, and that's temporary. But you're a damn fool — and that's permanent!'

A woman was arguing with an obviously inebriated man in the saloon bar. 'Stop telling me I remind you of your first wife!' she shouted. 'I *am* your first wife!'

You've got to admit — the government knows what it's doing. First they put a big tax on beer, wine and spirits. Then they raise all the other taxes and drive people to drink!

Two Irishmen were talking in a pub. 'When I'm dead and buried, Patrick,' said Michael, 'I want you to pour a bottle of the very best Irish whiskey over my grave.'

'I'll do that,' said Patrick. 'But do you mind if I pass it through me kidneys first?'

A man walked into a pub with a pet tiger on a leash. He ordered a pint of lager for himself and one for the tiger. They continued drinking for an hour or so and the tiger passed out. The man got up and started to leave the pub, and the barman shouted, 'Oi! You can't leave that lyin' there!'

And the man said, 'It's not a lion, it's a tiger.'

A fellow had been out on the razzle, and after the pubs had shut he spent the rest of the night in the company of a charming young blonde. He staggered into the bedroom at five in the morning to find his wife awake and waiting up for him. Trying to appear as sober as possible, he started to get undressed.

Suddenly his wife said, 'My God! Where are your underpants?'

The drunk glanced down blearily and then, thinking quickly, said, 'Good Lord! I've been robbed!'

Two inebriates were making their unsteady way home along the railway line. 'I never saw so many steps in my life!' muttered one of them.

'It's not the steps that bother me,' said the second. 'It's the low railing!'

A fellow who had imbibed rather too freely wandered into a cemetery late at night and fell into an open grave. His cries for help were heard by another homeward-bound drunk who came over to investigate.

'Get me out of here!' hollered the drunk in the grave. 'It's freezing down here!'

'I'm not surprised,' said the second drunk. 'They forgot to cover you up!'

Two drunks were on a pub crawl. Round about nine o'clock they ran out of money. 'I've got an idea,' said one. 'Lesh go over to my house and borrow shum money from my wife!'

So home they went, staggered upstairs to the bedroom, switched on the light, and there was the first drunk's wife in bed with a strange man. The first drunk didn't seem to be a bit upset about this, although his pal was considerably shocked. 'Hello, dear,' said the first drunk cheerfully. 'Shay, do you have any money for your loving hushband?'

'My purse is on the kitchen table downstairs,' snapped the wife. 'Now for heaven's sake get out of here!'

The two drunks made their way down to the kitchen and helped themselves. 'Oh boy!' said the first drunk, 'there's enough here for a couple of pints for me and a couple for you!'

'Yes, but what about that fellow up there with your wife?' asked his pal.

'To hell with him!' said the first drunk. 'Let him buy his own beer!'


Wife: What's the idea of getting home at this time in the morning?
Husband: What do you mean? I hurried home becaush I thought you might be loneshum, but I shee you've got [hic!] your twin shishter shtaying with you!


During the days of Prohibition in America, two moonshiners were discussing business. 'When I takes my liquor into town,' said one, 'I always drives mighty slow.'

'Why's that?' asked the second man.

'Well, you gotta age the stuff, ain't you!' was the reply.

'I'm drinking to forget,' said the sad drunk at the bar.
'To forget what?' asked the bartender.
'To forget I'm an alcoholic!'

Two Scotsmen were appearing in court, charged with being drunk and disorderly. 'How do you know they were drunk?' asked the judge.

'Well, sir,' said the constable, 'one of them had his wallet open and was throwing money away – and the other one was picking it up and giving it back.'

The temperance lecturer looked sternly at his audience and declared, 'I have lived in this town all my life. There are 123 pubs in this district and I can honestly say I've never been in one of them.'

'Which one is that?' said a voice from the back of the hall.

I understand there's a new organization called the AAAA – it's for people who are being driven to drink.

Late one evening, the door of the police station was pushed open and in staggered a chap who had obviously had one over the proverbial eight. 'Offisher,' he said to the duty policeman, 'do you remember me? My place wash burgled last week without anyone being woken up.'

'Yes, sir,' said the policeman. 'I remember.'

'Well,' said the drunk, 'could you put me in touch with the man that did it? I want to ask him how he got in without waking my wife.'

A fellow was travelling to work on the bus one morning and the conductor recognized him. 'Did you get home all right last night?' asked the conductor.

'Yes,' said the fellow. 'Why do you ask?'

'Because when you got up and gave that lady your seat, you two were the only people on the bus!'

One day, at lunch, W. C. Fields was suffering from an unusually severe hangover. 'Can I fix you an Alka-Seltzer, sir?' asked the waiter.

'No,' moaned Fields. 'I couldn't stand the noise!'

O'*Reilly:* Did you hear about O'Shaughnessy? He fell down a flight of stairs with a crate of Guinness and he didn't spill a drop!

O'*Rourke:* How did he manage that?

O'*Reilly:* He kept his mouth shut.

A white horse walked into a pub and said, 'A pint of lager please.' The barman served him and said, 'This is quite a coincidence — we've got a whisky here named after you.' And the horse said, 'What — Percy?'

A drunk on a bus was tearing a newspaper into small pieces and throwing them out of the window. 'What do you think you're doing?' asked the conductor.

'It's to scare away the elephants,' said the drunk.

'To scare away the elephants? There's no elephants around here!'

'I know,' said the drunk. 'Effective isn't it?'

After celebrating rather too freely, a fellow stumbled home at about one in the morning. His wife was sitting up in bed waiting for him. She heard him groping about downstairs and suddenly there was a tremendous crash and the sound of breaking glass. 'What on earth are you doing down there?' she shouted. And the husband bawled back, 'I'm just teaching the goldfish not to bark at me!'

Down in Kentucky, they like their whisky straight. One old-timer was handed a shot of rye. 'Blindfold me and hold my nose,' he said. 'If I see it or smell it, my mouth will water and dilute it!'

'Allow me to pour you another drink. I've heard you like good liquor.'
'Yes, I do — but pour me another one anyway.'

The husband had had a fine old time at the office Christmas Party. He made his unsteady way home at about one in the morning and, going up the front steps of his house, he tripped and fell, cutting his face. Once safely inside, he staggered into the bathroom to clean himself up, realizing that his wife would be bound to ask questions if she saw him bleeding all over the place.

The next morning at breakfast, the wife berated him for coming home drunk. 'Nonsense,' he protested. 'I was perfectly sober.'

'Well, in that case,' said the wife with a grim smile, 'how is it that the bathroom mirror has pieces of sticking plaster all over it?'

Three men were having a drink in a rather seedy pub. The place was infested with flies. One fly fell into the Englishman's beer and he carefully lifted it out with his fingers. Then a second fly fell into the Irishman's beer. The Irishman took no notice of it but went on drinking happily. When a third fly fell into the Scotsman's beer, he lifted it carefully, wrung it out into his beer, and carried on drinking.

Two British astronauts landed on the moon, and one of them went off to look for a pub.

'Any luck?' said his partner when he returned half an hour later.

'There's only one pub in the whole place,' said the first astronaut.

'Any good?' asked his pal.

'No!' said the first astronaut disgustedly. 'No atmosphere!'

Two drunks had wandered into the reading room of the British Library and one of them was avidly reading the world population statistics.

'Do you know,' he said to his mate, 'that every time I breathe, a man dies?'

The second drunk looked at him sympathetically and said, 'Have you tried chlorophyll tablets?'

Down in Cornwall, there's a pub where the bar is decorated with stuffed fish in glass cases. A drunk wandered round staring at these exhibits with interest. Suddenly he came to an enormous stuffed marlin in a huge case. After studying it carefully for a few moments, he said, 'The feller that caught that is a damn liar!'

A very happy gentleman left his West End club and started to make his uncertain way home to his flat in Piccadilly. Halfway through the journey, he bumped into a tree which was surrounded by a protective circle of iron rods. He clutched hold of these rods and went round three times, hand over hand. Then he stopped and shouted in a plaintive voice: 'Help! I'm trapped! Somebody let me out!'

A friend of mine bought one of those cassettes that help you to stop drinking while you're sleeping. He hasn't had a drink since — while he's sleeping.

A recent survey has shown that men sitting in bars are only there for one of two reasons. Either they have no wife to go home to — or they do.

Two fellows were on holiday in Ireland. Unused to the potency of Guinness, they were groping their way home along a lonely road one night, when they came upon what appeared to be a tombstone.

'We must have wandered into a cemetery,' muttered one. 'What does that tombstone say?' The other struck a match and peered closely at the object.

'Whoever he was, he lived to a ripe old age,' he said. 'Ninety-eight!' He struck another match and looked again. 'Seems like it was some fellow called "Miles from Dublin",' he said.

A fellow attending a cocktail party had had rather too much to drink. Not wishing to make a fool of himself, he said to the host, 'Though I may be slightly under the affluence of incohol, I'm not so think as you drunk I am!'

A drunk staggered on to a bus and sat down next to an elderly vicar. 'You may not know it,' said the vicar sternly, 'but you're going straight to hell!'

'Oh, my God!' said the drunk, leaping to his feet. 'Let me off! I'm on the wrong bus!'

## DRINKER'S DICTIONARY

WHISKY: the stuff that takes away the taste of water.

TEQUILA: the Gulp of Mexico.

TEETOTALLER: a person who adds up golf scores.

BEER: a drink that gives you a run for your money.

SUNDAY PUNCH: the drinks left over from Saturday night.

ALCOHOLIC: a fellow you don't like who drinks as much as you do.

ALCOHOLICS ANONYMOUS: a place where you can drink in secret.

ACUTE ALCOHOLIC: a pretty drunk.

Just before closing time, a flea dashed into a pub, ordered five double whiskys, drank them straight down, rushed into the street, jumped high in the air and fell flat on his face. 'Dammit!' he cried as he picked himself up. 'Who's moved my dog?'

Judge: You are charged with habitual drunkenness. What excuse have you got to offer?
Prisoner: Habitual thirst, your Honour.

I wouldn't say my wife drinks a lot but she once held up a ship launching for three hours. She wouldn't let go of the bottle.

A chap goes into a pub and the barman says, 'Good evening, sir. What is your pleasure?'

'Thank you very much. I'll have a Scotch and a box of matches, please.' He then puts 5p on the counter and drinks the Scotch.

'What's the 5p for?' asks the barman.

'For the matches. I didn't really want a drink but you asked me so nicely what my pleasure was.'

The barman begins to get cross. 'Look here, I was only being polite.'

The chap is adamant. 'I'm sorry but I refuse to pay.' He is barred from the pub.

Two weeks later he walks back in, and the barman shouts, 'Hey, you! Out! I told you I never wanted to see you again!' The chap refuses to leave.

'You must have me mixed up with somebody else,' he says. 'I've just come back after four months abroad.'

After a close look, the barman says, 'I can't understand it, sir. You must have a double.'

'Thanks,' says the man. 'And a box of matches as well, please.'

A fellow I know has a reputation for being something of an expert on wine. He only has to taste a glass of wine and he can tell you not only what it is and its vintage and year – he can also tell you who jumped on the grapes!

Doctors are always telling us that drinking shortens your life. Well, I've seen more old drunkards than old doctors.

A chap I know used to drink whisky and water which always made him drunk. He switched to brandy and water but that always made him drunk too. Then he changed to rum and water and that made him drunk. Now he's convinced that water is an intoxicant.

*Wife:* What do you mean coming home at this time in the morning! And another thing – you smell of whisky!
*Husband:* So would you, if you'd drunk as much of it as I have!

A fellow walked into the saloon bar of the Crown and Anchor and said to the barman, 'Mick, the wife's mother has passed on. Can you loan me £25 for a wreath?'

'We've only just opened,' said the barman, 'but I'll see what I can do.' He emptied the till and looked in his wallet but he could only come up with £21.

'That'll do,' said the customer. 'I'll take the other four quid in drinks.'

*Host*: Would you like some grapes?
*Guest*: No, thank you – I don't like taking my wine in pills!

A gentleman more than slightly sozzled was fumbling at his keyhole one evening when a policeman approached. 'Can I help you, sir?' asked the constable.

'No, no, thash all right,' the drunk mumbled. 'You jes' hold the housh still and I can manage.'

*First Drunk*: Do you know, when I was born, I only weighed a pound and a quarter!
*Second Drunk*: Good heavens! Did you live?
*First Drunk*: Did I live! I'll say I did! You ought to see me now!

A fellow, clearly under the influence, was sitting in the corner of a bar, slowly nodding his head back and forth, and saying, 'Tick . . . tock . . . tick . . . tock . . . tick . . . tock . . .' The barman went over to him and said, 'Are you all right, mate?'

'Yes, I'm all right,' said the drunk.

'Well, what are you doing?'

'Can't you see?' said the drunk. 'I'm a clock.'

'Oh, yeah?' said the barman sarcastically. 'OK – what time is it?'

The drunk said, 'Half past ten.'

'Oh, no it isn't,' said the barman, glancing at his wristwatch. 'It's quarter to eleven.'

'My God!' said the drunk. 'I must be slow! Ticktockticktock-ticktock . . . !'

*Mrs Malone:* I'm in a terrible state, Mrs Flanagan! Me husband's very ill and I can't get his medicine!

*Mrs Flanagan:* Why ever not?

*Mrs Malone:* The pubs are shut!

'And I suppose you've spent all your money!' shouted the wife as her husband staggered in at one in the morning on Christmas Eve.

'Now don't get upset, dear,' said the cheerful drunk. 'I have spent all my money, yes, but I bought something for the house!'

'And just what did you buy for the house that cost so much?' said his wife grimly.

'Eight rounds of drinks!' he beamed.

A drunk was staggering home one night when he tripped and fell against a shop window. Luckily, he was unhurt, but the window was shattered. As he picked himself up, he saw a policeman walking towards him, so he took to his heels and hared off down the road. The policeman gave chase and caught him easily.

'Oh, no, you don't!' said the policeman. 'I saw you breaking that window and running away!'

'I wasn't running away, offisher,' said the drunk. 'I was running home to get the money to pay the owner!'

'Drinking will shorten your life,' said the doctor. 'If you stop drinking, it will prolong your days.'

'You're right there, Doc,' said the patient. 'Last week, I went twenty-four hours without touching a drop, and I've never spent such a long day in my life!'

A fellow on holiday in Brighton developed cramp while out swimming. Some other bathers dragged him ashore and laid him on the beach. One of them produced a bottle of brandy and as he was unscrewing the top, the rescued swimmer gasped, 'Before you force that brandy down my throat, turn me over and get some of the water out of me!'

*Rag-and-Bone Man*: Got any empty beer bottles, lady?
*Lady of the House* (glaring at him frostily): Do I look as though I drink beer, my man!
*Rag-and-Bone Man*: Sorry, lady. Got any empty vinegar bottles?

My uncle was so drunk at his last birthday party that he lit the candles on his cake with one breath.

'Do you realize that you didn't get home until three a.m. this morning!' stormed the wife.
'Oh, no, dear,' said the husband, 'I'm sure you're wrong. I distinctly heard the dining-room clock strike one . . . several times!'

A drunk was hammering on the front door of a house at one o'clock in the morning. An upstairs window opened with a bang and an irate lady shouted down, 'What do you want?'
'Can you tell me where Dave Smith lives?' the drunk called up.
'What are you on about?' the woman shouted back. '*You're* Dave Smith!'
'I know,' said the drunk. 'But where does he live?'

Winston Churchill was once served a very weak whisky and soda at an official reception. 'Which did you put in first, waiter,' he asked, 'the whisky or the soda?'

'I put the whisky in first, sir,' said the waiter.

'Oh, well,' said Churchill. 'No doubt I'll come to it in due course.'

Two habitual drunks met on a train. They had already spent several hours in the buffet and had got through quite a few miniatures between them. They chatted happily for some time and then one said, 'You know, rail travel ish a marvelloush thing! I'm going to Edinburgh and you're going to London – and here we are, on the same train!'

A drunk was driving the wrong way down a one-way street when he was stopped by a policeman. 'Where do you think you're going?' demanded the policeman.

'I don't know,' muttered the drunk, 'but wherever it is, I must be terribly late – everyone else is coming home!'

Not drunk is he, who from the floor,
Can rise alone, and still drink more;
But drunk is he, who prostrate lies,
Without the power to drink or rise.

*Thomas Love Peacock*

*First Party Guest:* I shay, old boy, thish punch is a bit weak, isn't it?

*Second Party Guest:* You're dipping your cup into the goldfish bowl, old man!

Halfway through the office Christmas party, at which the drinks had flowed freely, the sales manager started going round and wishing everybody goodnight. 'Surely you're not leaving yet?' said the managing director.

'No,' said the sales manager, 'but I'm saying goodnight now while I still know who everybody is.'

A fine beer is like a fine woman — it has a good head, a full body, and makes you want to come back for more.

An elderly and rather infirm lady had engaged a new maid. 'Now sometimes,' she explained, 'you will have to help me up the stairs at night.'

'I quite understand, ma'am,' said the maid. 'I likes a few drinks meself from time to time.'

One day in late December, on a date I don't remember,
I was stumbling home, my head held high with pride,
When my feet began to stutter, and I lay down in the gutter,
And a pig came up and lay down at my side.
As we lay there in contentment, without rancour or resentment,
A lady passing by was heard to say,
'You can tell when someone boozes by the company he chooses,'
And the pig got up and slowly walked away.

Jim: What did the doctor say about your drinking?
Joe: He told me to limit myself to one drink a day.
Jim: And are you carrying out his instructions?
Joe: Oh, yes. Right now, I'm working on the 5th of September, 1998.

'Why does it take you so long to mix a martini?'
'I use sloe gin.'

'Well, dear,' said the husband at breakfast, 'you can't complain that I made any noise coming in last night.'
'No,' said the wife, 'but the fellows carrying you did.'

The cost of living is really a serious problem these days. The necessities of life cost five times what they did ten years ago − and half the time, they aren't even fit to drink.

A fellow obviously the worse for wear was standing by the automatic sandwich machine on Victoria Station. He was inserting money as fast as he could and soon had a great pile of sandwiches in his arms. The station manager walked over and said, 'I should stop if I were you, sir. I think you've got enough now.'
'Stop!' said the drunk. 'Are you crazy? You want me to stop when I'm on a winning streak!'

Two fellows staggered pale-faced into a pub. They had a couple of stiff ones and then one of them said to the barman, 'How big would you say a penguin was?'

The barman said, 'Oh, I don't know. About two and a half feet, I suppose.'

The fellow turned to his pal and said, 'There you are! I told you it was a nun we just ran over!'


Joe: Is there any alcohol in cider?
Moe: Inside who?


As Oliver Reed once said, 'I know my capacity for drink, but I keep getting drunk before I reach it!'


Vicar: You should give up drinking! I've told you before
    – drink is your worst enemy!
Drunk: You did, vicar, you did – but didn't you also tell me
    we should love our enemies?


Two drunks decided to visit a sauna bath. After about half an hour, one drunk said to the other, 'I've had enough of this!'

'Well, go home then,' said his pal.

'I will,' said the first, 'as soon as this damn fog lifts!'

*Professor:* I refuse to begin my lecture until the room settles down!

*Voice from the Back:* Why don't you go home and sleep it off?

A friend of mine is not exactly an alcoholic but he's the only guy I know who has rheumatism of the hip from putting wet change in his pocket.

Two drunks were staggering down the street. One of them said, 'Do you know, we jush pashed a feller who looks just like you!'

The other drunk said, 'Lesh go back and see if it was me!'

The fellow leaning up against the bar was obviously well under the influence. He asked the barman where the gents was and the barman pointed it out to him, calling jokingly as the drunk staggered off, 'Have one for me, will you!'

A few minutes later, the drunk stumbled back. As he reached the bar, he said, 'Dammit! I forgot to have one for you!' Off he went again, returning five minutes later, muttering under his breath.

'Anything wrong?' asked the barman.

'You didn't want to go at all!' said the drunk.

A husband was leaving the house for his usual evening session at the local. 'What would you do,' asked his wife, 'if you came home one night and found me in bed with a strange man?'

Said the husband, 'I'd break his white stick and shoot his guide dog.'

'Just because the accused was holding a fifteen-foot ladder,' said the magistrate, 'that doesn't mean he was drunk.'

'No, sir,' said the arresting officer, 'but he was trying to climb up it!'

A fellow in a high state of intoxication called round to see an artist friend. The painter had just completed a landscape and the drunk looked at it for several moments in admiration. At length he said, 'Brilliant! Absholutely brilliant! How on earth do you manage to get the trees to wave so realishtically?'

A fellow was just about to enter his favourite pub when he noticed a nun peering in through the window. On the spur of the moment, he asked her if she would like to come inside, just to see what a pub was like. After a few weak protests, the nun agreed and they went inside together. They sat down at a table and a barmaid came over. 'What can I get you?' she asked.

'I'll have a double Scotch,' said the man. 'Can I tempt you to a little something, Sister?'

'Well, I don't know,' said the nun dubiously. She glanced at the price list on the wall and said, 'All right, then – I'll try one of those – er, "mar-tinys".'

The barmaid smiled and crossed to the counter. 'A double Scotch and a "mar-tiny",' she said.

'Oh, no,' said the bartender. 'Don't tell me that nun's in here again!'

After making the rounds of all the pubs in the neighbourhood, an Irishman returned home to find that he had mislaid his umbrella. The next day, he called in at all the fifteen pubs he had visited to see if they had it. He had no luck in the first fourteen, but found his umbrella in the fifteenth. 'You're the only honest barman in town!' he said. 'All the others said they hadn't got it!'

A lot of people think my uncle is a drunkard but it's not true. It's just that a few years ago he donated his body to science and he's preserving it in alcohol until they want it.

Two fellows were talking in a pub. 'What's your great ambition in life?' asked one.
'To own my own pub,' said the second. 'What's yours?'
'Thanks,' said the first man. 'I'll have a double brandy.'

A customer in a bar complained that his beer was cloudy. 'There's nothing wrong with the beer,' said the barman. 'It's the dirty glass that gives it that appearance.'

There was a young lady of Kent,
    Who said that she knew what it meant
When men asked her to dine,
Gave her cocktails and wine;
She knew what it meant – but she went!

A Scottish laird had given his favourite gillie a hunting cap with ear-flaps as a Christmas present. On the first shoot after Christmas, the laird noticed that the gillie wasn't wearing the cap and asked him why. 'I've not worn it since the accident, sir,' said the gillie.

'What accident?' asked the laird.

'Well, sir,' said the gillie, 'I was wearing it with the ear-flaps down when a fellow offered me a dram − and I didna hear him!'

A doctor was advising a woman whose husband was an alcoholic. 'Has he ever tried Alcoholics Anonymous?' he asked.

'I expect so,' said the woman grimly. 'He'll drink anything!'

It was the end of harvest time and the farmer, a man not noted for generosity, gave his head man a glass of beer. The farm hand drank the beer but said nothing so the farmer asked if it was all right. 'Just,' he replied.

'What do you mean "just"?' asked the farmer.

'Well, sir,' said the farm hand, 'if it had been any better, you wouldn't have given it to me − and if it had been any worse, I couldn't have drunk it.'

Two Irishmen were appearing in court on a charge of being drunk and disorderly. 'Where do you live?' asked the magistrate.

'No fixed abode, yer Honour,' said the first drunk.

'And where do you live?' asked the magistrate, looking at the second Irishman.

'In the flat above him, yer Honour.'

41

A vicar was returning home late one night when he spotted a drunk staggering along the street. He knew the man and he very kindly helped him to his front door. 'Will you come inshide, Reverend?' asked the drunk.

'Well, it's getting rather late . . .' said the vicar.

'Pleash, Reverend,' begged the drunk. 'I jush want the wife to shee who I've been out with tonight.'

Two Irishmen were sharing a flat in London. One Saturday, one of them went out to do the shopping and returned with five crates of Guinness and a loaf of bread. 'Are we having a party, Mick?' asked his friend.

'No. Why?' said Mick.

'Well, what's all the bread for?' said his mate.

'Do you, or do you not admit that you were drunk last night?' demanded the irate wife.

'I only had just the one glass, dear,' said the husband. 'The trouble was, they kept filling it up again!'

At a country auction in a small West Country town, a great deal of interest was shown in an antique whisky bottle. It was knocked down for £75 to a bidder from Bristol. As he collected his purchase, a farmer standing next to him looked at it and exclaimed, 'Good God! It's empty!'

A bishop was travelling by train to an important meeting of the synod in the north of England. A chap came back after a happy hour or two in the buffet car and sat down unsteadily opposite the cleric. He stared for some moments at the bishop, resplendent in his black costume and gaiters. Then, leaning across, he said, 'Are you a curate?'

The bishop, amused, said, 'Well . . . I was a curate once but . . .'

'Say no more,' the drunk interrupted. 'I understand. What happened? It was the drinking, was it?'

W C. Fields used to carry a large cocktail shaker with him wherever he went. He always maintained that it was filled with pineapple juice. Needless to say, nobody believed him! One day, while filming, a cameraman secretly got hold of the cocktail shaker, emptied it out, and refilled it with real pineapple juice. Some time later, when Fields came on to the set, he took a hearty swig and shouted, 'Who's been putting pineapple juice in my pineapple juice!'

The party was in full swing when a fellow clutching a full pint of beer approached a chap standing quietly in the corner. 'Do you drink?' he said.

'No, I don't,' said the second chap.

'Good. Hold my beer a minute while I tie my shoelace.'

The drunk handed over his bus pass and the conductor said, 'This is out of date, pal. Today's Saturday and this pass expired on Thursday.'

'So what?' said the drunk belligerently. 'It's not my fault if the bus is two days late!'

Two fellows drinking in a bar called the proprietor over and asked him if he would settle a bet for them. He agreed and the first fellow said, 'How many pints are there in a quart — is it two or four?'

'Two pints in a quart,' said the proprietor.

'Thanks a lot,' said the chap, and the two of them finished their drinks and went out. Five minutes later, they were back again, and the barmaid said, 'What'll it be, gents?'

'Two pints, please,' said the first fellow. 'And these are on the house.' The barmaid looked doubtful so the fellow called out to the proprietor, who was standing at the other end of the bar, 'You did say two pints, didn't you?'

And the proprietor shouted back, 'That's right — two pints!'


A man with a serious drinking problem was advised by his doctor to give up alcohol altogether. To help him do this, the doctor suggested that every time he felt the need for a drink, he should have something to eat instead. The drinker adopted this suggestion and it seemed to work.

He had to go away on business and one night, in his hotel room, he heard strange noises coming from the room next door. He went out into the corridor and peeped through the keyhole. To his horror, he saw a man standing on a chair, on the point of hanging himself from a rope attached to the ceiling. He rushed downstairs to reception and shouted, 'Quick — there's a fellow in the next room trying to hang himself. For God's sake, give me a plate of ham and eggs!'

After a day at the races, two drunks booked a twin-bedded room at a small hotel. They staggered up to the room and, still fully dressed, they switched off the light and both lay down on the same bed. After a while, the first drunk said, 'I shay, I think there's someone lying on thish bed with me!'

'Yesh, and there's someone in my bed, too!' said the second drunk.

'Well, lesh kick 'em out!' said the first drunk, and a terrific struggle ensued. Finally, the first drunk said, 'I got my fellow out!'

'I couldn't handle mine,' said the second drunk, 'he pushed me out on the floor!'

'Never mind,' said his pal. 'You jesh come and sleep with me!'


A fellow obviously the worse for wear got on a number 73 bus and sat near the driver. All through the journey, he kept pestering the driver with inane remarks and questions. Finally, the driver said, 'Why don't you go and sit upstairs. You'll get a much better view from up there.'

So the drunk staggered up the stairs but within a few minutes he was back down again.

'What's the matter?' asked the driver. 'Don't you like it up there?'

'No,' said the drunk. 'It's not safe. There's no driver!'


A fellow with a serious drinking problem managed to get himself a job in the china and glassware department of a large London store. He hadn't been there an hour when he let a valuable porcelain vase slip through his trembling hands and smash on the floor. 'That vase was worth £500!' said the manager. 'I'm going to have to deduct £5 a week from your wages to cover the cost.'

'Great!' said the new employee. 'My wife will be pleased! It's the first steady job I've had in years!'

There is an old Arab legend that relates how the Devil appeared before a man and said, 'You are about to die. There are three possible ways you can avoid this. Either you can kill your servant; or you can beat your wife; or you can drink this bottle of wine.'

The man said, 'I couldn't possibly kill my good and faithful servant – and I love my wife too much to beat her. I'll drink the bottle of wine.' So he drank the wine. And then, being drunk, he beat his wife, and when his servant tried to stop him, he killed him.

A fellow at a party ran into his ex-wife. Mellowed by several drinks, he suggested that they try again to make a go of things, and that they start off by going to bed together. 'Over my dead body!' she sneered.

'Oh,' said the ex-husband, 'I see you haven't changed a bit!'

After many years of hard drinking, two Scotsmen decided to become teetotallers. They thought it wise, however, to keep a bottle of whisky in the kitchen in case of illness. After three weeks, one of them began to weaken and he said, 'I'm afraid, MacTavish, that I'm not feelin' very well.'

'You're too late, McNab,' said the other. 'I was very sick myself all day yesterday!'

A Scotsman was sitting quietly in a pub when a waiter spilled a tray of drinks all over him. It was the first time the drinks had been on him for thirty years.

The victorious rugby team had been in the pub all night, drinking, fooling around, breaking up the furniture and singing continuously at the tops of their voices. Gradually they drifted away, leaving six stalwarts who staggered out at closing time. As they crowded into their battered old Volkswagen, the team captain said, 'You'd better drive, Jimmy – you're far too drunk to sing!'

Little Andrew MacFarlane asked his father, 'Daddy – what exactly is Scotch mist?'

'It's when a man asks you to have a drink, laddie,' replied his father, 'and you don't hear him!'

A man walked into a bar in the Catholic area of Belfast with a crocodile on a leash. 'Do you serve Protestants here?' he asked.

'Certainly,' said the barman. 'We're not prejudiced.'

'Good,' said the man. 'Give me a pint of Guinness and a couple of Protestants for my crocodile.'

Late one night there was a knock on the door of a suburban house. The lady of the house opened her bedroom window and saw a group of half-a-dozen men on the doorstep. 'What do you want?' she shouted.

'Are you Mrs Williams?' one of them shouted back.

'Yes, I am.'

'Well, come on down and pick out Mr Williams – the rest of us want to go home.'

It had been a spectacular party and the young couple were taking a late lunch. 'I was really well away last night,' said the young man. 'I can't remember a thing! Was it you I made love to out on the patio last evening?'

'I really don't know,' said the young woman. 'About what time?'

'I hear you've been drying out on a health farm. How was it?'
'Terrible! I had to live for two weeks on nothing but food and water!'

A drunk walked into a bar and shouted, 'Happy New Year, everybody!'

'What are you talking about?' said the barman. 'It's the first of April!'

'Oh my God!' said the drunk. 'My wife'll kill me when I get home! I've been out for three months!'

Every night a chap came into a bar and ordered two single whiskys. After a few weeks of this, the barman asked him why he didn't just order a double. 'Well,' the fellow replied, 'I order two singles because one's for my mate in Manchester.'

Then one night he came in and asked for a single whisky. 'What about your friend?' asked the barman. 'Did he die or something?'

'No, nothing like that,' said the chap. 'It's just that I'm on the wagon.'

A drunk was weaving his unsteady way home one evening when he happened to pass the window of a wine merchant's where a wine-tasting party was in progress. He pressed his nose to the window and saw a man tasting glasses of wine. After taking a sip from each, he spat the wine out. After he had done this five or six times, the drunk walked off muttering, 'You'll never get me in *that* pub!'

I don't know about you, but I much prefer telling my troubles to a bartender than to a psychiatrist. He's cheaper; he's more accessible; and he never tells me to give up drinking.

## THE DRINKER'S GUIDE TO COCKTAILS

BERMUDA COCKTAIL: three gulps and your breath will come in short pants.

SUBMARINE SPECIAL: one and you go under for the night.

SOUTH PACIFIC: one sip and you'll want Samoa.

BACK TO SCHOOL SPECIAL: one drink and you're in a class by yourself.

LINOLEUM COCKTAIL: one drink and you're flat on the floor.

KILLARNEY COCKTAIL: two sips and you turn green.

JEKYLL AND HYDE: just one and you're a new man.

DAVID AND GOLIATH SPECIAL: one small one and you're stoned.

CARD TABLE SPECIAL: one small sip and your legs fold up.

WHISTLER'S MOTHER: one of these and you're off your rocker.

IRISH COCKTAIL: half whiskey with another half added.

A long-suffering wife was about to berate her husband for staggering home at three a.m. 'Before you begin,' he warned her, 'I want you to know I been sittin' up with a sick friend.'

'A likely story,' mocked the wife. 'What was his name?'

The husband gave this problem deep thought and then announced triumphantly, 'He was so sick, he couldn't tell me.'

A drunk staggered home one night after an intensive pub crawl. He stumbled upstairs and into the bathroom, finishing up in the shower. He groped about and accidentally turned on the water. As he stood there getting drenched, his wife came in to see what all the noise was about and began to give him a real ticking-off, calling him all the names under the sun. 'You're absholutely right, my dear,' said the drunk. 'But open the door and let me in, will you − it's raining like hell out here!'

A drunk was staggering home one night with one foot on the pavement and one foot in the gutter. 'Thash funny,' he muttered, looking down. 'Both my legs were the same length this morning!'

An Englishman was entertaining a party of Americans at his club in Pall Mall. The Americans started swapping anecdotes and one said, 'I stayed out so late drinking last night that on the way home, I met myself going to the office!'

The Americans roared with laughter, but the Englishman only smiled dubiously. 'Don't you get it?' said the American.

'Yes, I think so,' said the Englishman. 'Of course, you would never have recognized yourself in that condition.'

A doleful-looking customer went to the bar and ordered six whiskies. The barman poured them out for him in six glasses. 'Now line them up in front of me, will you?' asked the customer. He then paid for them and told the barman to keep the change. He swallowed down the contents of the first glass in the line and then repeated the process with the third and fifth glasses. Then he turned and walked away.

'Excuse me, sir,' the barman called, 'you've left three glasses untouched.'

'Yes, I know,' said the customer. 'My doctor said he didn't mind me taking the odd drink.'

A vicar received a present from one of his parishioners in the form of a bottle of cherries preserved in brandy. He wrote the following letter of thanks: *Thank you very much for your most welcome gift and particularly for the spirit in which it was given.*

A distinguished-looking gentleman, obviously under the influence, hammered on the bar and demanded, 'What do I have to do to get a little service around here? Have you the faintest idea who I am?'

'No, sir,' said the barman, 'but you sit right there and I'll try to find out for you.'

*Doctor:* I'm afraid you're suffering from hydropsy.
*Patient:* What's that?
*Doctor:* Too much water in the body.
*Patient:* But I've never touched a drop of water in my life!
*Doctor:* Perhaps it was all those ice cubes, then.

Two fellows returned to their hotel in a highly intoxicated state. One of them seemed distinctly unwell so his friend got him into bed and had the hotel receptionist call a doctor. The doctor arrived and examined the chap in bed. 'Do you see any pink elephants in the room?' he asked.

'No,' said the chap.

'Any little green men?'

'No.'

'Well, you'll be all right,' said the doctor. 'Just get a good night's sleep and you'll be fine in the morning.'

After the doctor had gone, the second chap went down and spoke to the receptionist. 'I'm afraid my pal's in a worse state than I thought,' he said. 'The doctor asked him if he could see any pink elephants or little green men, and he said no. And do you know, the damn room was full of them!'

Two fellows had been propping up the bar all evening. Just before closing time, one of them said, 'Lesh have one more drink and then go out and pick up a couple of girls!'

'No,' said the other. 'I've got more than I can handle in that department at home!'

'OK,' said the first chap. 'Then lesh have one more drink, and go round to your place!'

Host: What can I get you?
Guest: I fancy something tall, cool and full of gin.
Host: Come over and meet the wife.

I never drink water myself. If it can rust iron, just think what it can do to your insides!

54

A friend of mine has switched to drinking whisky and carrot juice. He still gets just as drunk but he can see to find his way home much better now.

The horse and mule live thirty years
And nothing know of wines and beers.
The goats and sheep at twenty die,
With never a taste of Scotch or rye.
The cow drinks water by the ton,
And at eighteen is mostly done.
The dog at sixteen cashes in
Without the aid of rum or gin.
The cat in milk and water soaks
And then in twelve short years it croaks.
The sober, modest, bone-dry hen
Lays eggs for nogs, then dies at ten.
The animals are strictly dry,
They sinless live and swiftly die.
While sinful, ginful, rum-soaked men
Survive for three score years and ten.
And some of us, though mighty few,
Stay pickled till we're ninety-two.

A Scottish doctor was asked what treatment he would prescribe for a patient with a head cold. 'Give him a couple of drams of whisky and send him to bed,' he said.

'But what if he's a teetotaller?' enquired the questioner.

'Why, man,' said the doctor, 'he wouldna be worth saving!'

An alcoholic big-game hunter was regaling his friends with an account of his recent trip through the African jungle. 'We almost ran out of food,' he said, 'and our stocks of whisky, gin, rum and vodka had all gone.'

'But surely you had water?' said one of his listeners.

'Oh, yes,' said the explorer. 'But it was no time to be thinking of taking a bath.'

A drunk wandered into a watchmakers and asked to see some clocks. 'This is a nice one,' said the assistant. 'It's an eight-day clock.'

'Wash 'at mean?' said the drunk.

'It means it runs for eight days without winding,' said the assistant.

'You don't shay!' said the drunk. 'How long does it run if you do wind it?'

An inebriate wandered into a small pub in a remote part of Wales and shouted to the assembled company, 'John Major has a face like the back end of a sheep!' The locals rose as one man and threw him out. As he lay on the pavement, bruised and battered, the drunk said, 'I didn't think they'd all be Tory supporters round these parts.'

'They're not,' said a passer-by. 'They're sheep farmers.'

An old Scotsman was very ill and he called in his friends to have a last drink with him. One drink led to another but at last the old man said he had had enough.

'I wouldna want to go to Heaven smelling of whisky,' he said.

'Aw, come on, Sandy,' said one of his pals. 'If ye dinna smell of whisky, they'll no recognize ye!'

'You'll have no objection to a drink, I suppose?'
    'I've never had one before.'
'What — a drink?'
'No — an objection!'

Q: In which month of the year do the Irish drink the least Guinness?
    A: February.

A worker on a building site in Dublin had had a drop too much of the hard stuff. He slipped and fell six floors to the street below. 'Did the fall hurt you at all?' said a sympathetic passer-by.

'No,' said the befuddled Irishman. 'The fall didn't hurt at all. It was hitting the pavement that did it.'

There's a new organization called Teetotallers Anonymous. Whenever you feel like giving up the drink, you give them a call and they send two drunks round to talk you out of it.

A drunk staggered into a cocktail lounge and placed a live lobster on the bar counter. 'Thish ish for you,' he said to the bartender. 'In recognition of your faithful service, and for giving me some of the best evenings of my life.'

'Thanks,' said the bartender. 'That's very nice of you. I'll take him home for dinner.'

'No, no, don't do that!' said the drunk. 'He's had his dinner. Take him to the pictures.'

'I hear your husband's taken up yoga. Has it helped him with his drinking problem?'

'In one way, yes. Now he can drink standing on his head.'

'I see your hand's bandaged. What happened?'

'Oh, just a little bit of trouble at the local last night. Couple of fellows couldn't hold their liquor and got into a fight. One of them accidentally stepped on my hand.'

The wedding was proceeding quite satisfactorily except for one thing. The groom was blind drunk! 'Don't you think it would be better if he came back when he's sober?' said the vicar to the bride.

'The trouble is,' said the bride tearfully, 'he won't come at all when he's sober.'

A drunk was walking home in London one night when he saw a group of workmen digging a big hole in the middle of the street. 'Whatcha doing?' he asked.

'Building an extension to the Metropolitan Line,' said the foreman.

'The Underground?' asked the drunk.

'Yes.'

'When do you expect to finish it?'

'Oh, in about eighteen months' time.'

'Aw, to hell with it!' said the drunk. 'I'll take a taxi!'

The customer was chatting to the landlord down at the Rose and Crown when he noticed the landlord's dog lying on the floor of the bar, licking his private parts. The customer said jokingly, 'I wish I could do that!'

'Well,' said the landlord, 'give him a biscuit and he might let you.'

A fellow walks into a pub with a couple of friends. 'Barman,' he says, 'three pints of lager and three double Scotches – oh, and three large brandies.' Then, turning to his companions, he says, 'Now – what are you two having?'

'I say, waiter,' said the gent in the posh restaurant, 'is this Burgundy the '82 or the '87?'

'Can't you tell the difference?' said the waiter.

'No, I can't,' said the diner.

'Then what the 'ell does it matter!' snapped the waiter.

The phone rang in Dooley's living-room. When he picked it up, a voice at the other end said, 'Dooley? This is McCarthy. Come on over – we're having a party!'

'I can't,' said Dooley. 'I've got a bad case of laryngitis here.'

'Oh, bring it over,' said McCarthy. 'This lot'll drink anything!'

Dignity is the one thing you can't preserve in alcohol.

A fellow was walking down a dark street one night when a drunk jumped out with a gun in his hand. 'Stop!' cried the drunk, and he pulled a bottle out of his pocket. Pointing the gun at the unfortunate passer-by, he thrust the bottle at him and said, 'Take a drink of thish!'

The poor chap took a good swig and then spat it out, saying, 'This stuff tastes awful!'

'I know, I know,' said the drunk. 'Now you hold the gun on me while I take a swallow!'

A party of deaf mutes was sitting in the corner of the bar using sign language. Faster and faster their fingers flew and they became more and more excited. Finally the landlord went over and asked them to leave. 'What did you do that for?' asked a customer. 'They weren't causing a nuisance.'

'I've told them a dozen times,' said the landlord. 'I don't allow singing in this bar!'

'I hear they had a beer-drinking contest in your local last night. Did you win?'

'No – but I came in sickened.'

'I think I'll mix myself a whisky, soda and starch.'

'Starch? Why starch?'

'I feel like a good stiff drink.'

An Irishman had been visiting friends for dinner. As it was late when he left for home, somewhat the worse for drink, they lent him a torch so he could find his way. About an hour later, there was a knock on the door, and there stood Patrick. 'I found me way home all right,' he said. 'So I've just brought your torch back.'

Two fellows in a pub had just ordered a round of drinks. As the barman brought them over to their table, one of them said, 'Look here, I've been staying with you for a week now and you've paid for everything, food, outings, theatre visits. Fair's fair. I can't let you pay for these drinks.'
'Well . . .' said his mate.
'No, no, I insist! I'll toss you for who pays.'

Did you hear about the fellow who arrived home late one night after a drinking party and tried to climb into the grandfather clock to phone his wife to say he'd been detained on business?

'I hear you've been drinking whisky for three weeks to cure your rheumatism?'
'That's right.'
'I can give you a cure for rheumatism if you like.'
'Shut up! I don't want to hear it!'

Two women were talking over lunch. 'I'm feeling a lot easier now about my husband,' said one.

'How's that, dear?' asked her friend.

'Well, I was always afraid that when he came home drunk each night, he might fall in the river and drown. But now that he's been made a magistrate, a policeman always brings him home.'

The fellow on the other end of the police station telephone was obviously well under the influence and over the limit. 'Offisher!' he blustered, 'come at once! Someone's pinched half my car! They've taken the dashboard, the steering wheel and all the foot pedals!' The sergeant promised to send a man round at once. No sooner had he put the phone down than it rang again. 'Ish me again!' said the drunk. 'Don't bother to come round. I got in the back seat by mishtake!'

A drunk was staggering down the street when he bumped into a well-dressed lady. Straightening himself up he said, 'Lady, you're the ugliest-looking woman I ever saw!'

'And you,' said the lady haughtily, 'are the drunkest man I ever saw!'

'Ah, yes,' replied the drunk, 'but in the morning, I'll be sober!'

The village policeman was ambling down the main street one evening. He arrived at the local pub where some of the old villagers were sitting on a bench enjoying their pints. Lying in the middle of the road with an empty whisky bottle by his side was an old fellow who was obviously completely oblivious to his surroundings. ''Allo, 'allo!' said the constable. 'This man's drunk! I shall have to lock him up.'

''E ain't drunk,' said one of the locals on the bench. 'I just seen 'is fingers move!'

The sales representative had been drinking in the bar of his hotel all evening. He had struck up a conversation with a delightful young lady who had matched him drink for drink, and round about midnight he suggested that she come up to his room. She agreed readily and as they were undressing, he said, 'I can't get over how young you look! Just how old are you?'

'Thirteen,' said the girl.

'Thirteen!' exclaimed the rep. 'Oh, my God! Quick – get your clothes on and get out of here!'

'What's the matter?' said the girl. 'You superstitious or something?'

The wife was understandably annoyed when her husband arrived home blind drunk at one in the morning. 'I could forgive you if it was the first time,' she said, 'but you came home in the same condition on the 8th of January 1952!'

During the Prohibition years in America, a certain homesteader in Alabama was arrested for selling alcohol illegally. He was hauled into court but luckily he had provided himself with a good defence lawyer. This lawyer put the accused in the dock and said, 'Ladies and gentlemen of the jury, take a good, long look at the defendant.'

The jury stared in silence at the homesteader's ruddy complexion and purple nose. 'I ask you,' said the lawyer, 'in all honesty – do you think he looks like a man who would sell a drink if he had it?'

It took the jury less than a minute to bring in a verdict of 'Not guilty'.

*Policeman:* Hey, you! You can't stand on the edge of the pavement in that condition!

*Drunk:* Oh yes I can, offisher! I've been standing here for an hour an' I haven't fallen off yet!


A friend of mine has just joined Alcoholics Anonymous. Now whenever he visits one of the local pubs, he goes in disguise.


'Do you ever suffer from headaches?' the doctor said to the alcoholic.

'Yes, sometimes,' said his patient.

'How often?' asked the doctor.

'Well, they come on about once a week, and last a fortnight.'


'You know, it's a funny thing, Brown,' said one drunk to another in the saloon bar of the local one night. 'Everybody says you're the spitting image of Jones. I don't think you look a bit like him. Do you?'

'No, I don't,' said his mate. 'But as a matter of fact, I *am* Jones.'

A drunken guest at a funeral wake rose unsteadily to his feet to make a speech in honour of the dear departed. 'Ladies and gentlemen,' he said in slurred tones, 'I would like to propose a toast to the bride and groom!'

The man next to him whispered, 'Sit down, you fool – it's a wake, not a wedding!'

'Well, never mind,' said the drunk cheerfully. 'Whatever it is, it's a hell of a party!'



A fellow walked into a pub and ordered a pint of bitter. He took one mouthful and then spat it out all over the bar counter. The landlord was furious, but the fellow apologized profusely. 'I'm so ashamed,' he said. 'I just can't help it! It's a sort of impulse that just comes over me when I take a drink. I can't tell you how sorry and ashamed I am!'

'Well, just get out of here and don't come back,' said the landlord. 'And if I were you, I'd go and see a psychiatrist. You need professional help.'

A few months later, the door of the pub opened and in walked the same man. 'Oh, it's you!' said the landlord. 'I thought I told you I didn't want to see you in here again.'

'It's quite all right,' said the customer. 'I took your advice and went to a psychiatrist, and now I'm completely cured!'

Somewhat mollified, the landlord said, 'Well, all right, then. But no tricks now – what'll you have?'

'A pint of bitter, please,' said the man. The landlord served him and he took one mouthful and spat it out over the bar counter. The landlord was livid.

'I thought you said you were cured!' he shouted.

'Oh, I am, I am,' said the customer. 'I don't feel one little bit ashamed now!'

Two strangers got to chatting in the pub. It turned out that one of them was on a visit from Manchester. 'I've got a brother in Manchester,' said the other chap. 'Done very well for himself. His name's Don Smith – runs a big engineering firm. He's got pots of money. If you run into him, tell him you met me and say I'm having a bit of a tough time of it at the moment, what with the recession and all, and a little financial help wouldn't come amiss.'

Several double whiskies later, he said, 'Shay, if you see that brother of mine, tell him I'm OK, will you? Doing fine, nothing to worry about!'

They moved on to brandies and soda, and after consuming several of these, the first chap said, 'If you see anything of that brother of mine when you get home, tell him I'm coining it in an' if he needs any help financially, he can count on me!'


The door of the pub swung open and in walked a small dog. 'Large gin and tonic, please,' he said. The barman served him, he drank it down, left some money on the counter, and walked out.

One of the customers said, 'What an extraordinary thing!' 'Yes,' said the barman. 'He usually has a double Scotch.'


A celebrated professor was giving a talk on nuclear physics. One member of his audience was quite obviously drunk but seemed to be following the lecture with great interest. After the talk was finished, the drunk walked up to the professor and asked him to explain a rather complicated point in his address. 'I'll be pleased to answer your question,' said the professor, 'but don't you think it would be better to make an appointment and come and see me when you're sober?'

'No, no,' said the drunk earnestly. 'I want to know now. When I'm sober, I won't give a damn!'

On an Intercity Express, a man rushed into one of the carriages and said urgently, 'Has anyone got any brandy? A woman's fainted in the next carriage.' One of the passengers produced a flask and the fellow grabbed it and took a good long swig. 'Thanks,' he said, handing the flask back. 'It always upsets me to see a woman faint.'

The host at a cocktail party had made sure that everybody had a drink, with the exception of a rather severe-looking lady standing on her own. 'May I have a glass of wine?' she asked.

'Why, of course,' said the host. 'But I thought you were the secretary of the Temperance Society?'

'No,' she said. 'I'm the secretary of the Safe Sex Society.'

'Oh, I see,' said the host. 'I knew there was something I shouldn't offer you!'

'Way back during Prohibition,' said the old-timer, 'we made some of the best moonshine likker in Kentucky! We used to put in a hundred bushels of corn, a hundred bushels of wheat, and a hundred pounds of noodles. That way, when the revenuers came around, they thought we wuz making soup!'

The barman was tidying up one night after closing time when he came across an old fellow lying flat out under a table. He propped him up on a chair, looked through his pockets and found his name and address. Then he carried the old chap out to his car, drove him home, and lugged him up to the front door. He propped him up against the wall, and the fellow immediately slithered to the ground. The old chap's wife opened the door and said, 'Oh, you've brought him home! But where's his wheelchair?'

A fellow walked into a pub with a little Yorkshire terrier and said, 'Pint of lager, please.'

The dog said, 'I'll have the same.'

'Are you a ventriloquist?' asked the barman.

'No,' the chap said. 'He can really talk. And he can do all sorts of things – he can even run messages for me.'

The barman was amazed. 'Could he go round to the newsagents and get me a packet of tobacco?' he asked.

'Certainly,' said the customer. So the barman gave the dog a five-pound note and off it trotted.

After about an hour, there was no sign of the dog, so the customer and the barman went out to look for him. They found him in a nearby field, having a wonderful time with a little lady poodle. 'I'm surprised at you!' said his owner. 'You've never done anything like this before!'

'No,' said the dog. 'I've never had the money before!'


According to the British Medical Council, it's all right to drink like a fish – as long as you drink what a fish drinks.


A student at Cambridge was called in to see the Dean. 'I understand,' said the Dean, 'that you have a barrel of beer in your room which, as you well know, is contrary to the rules of the college.'

'Well, sir,' said the student, 'that is true – but the fact is, I have a very weak constitution and the doctor told me that I should drink beer regularly in order to build up my strength.'

The Dean looked sceptical. 'And are you getting stronger?' he asked.

'Oh, yes, sir,' said the student. 'When I took delivery of that barrel, I could hardly lift it. But now, after only a couple of weeks, I can roll it round the room quite easily.'

Three fellows found themselves with a raging thirst and not a penny between them. They worked out a plan to overcome this little difficulty and headed for the nearest pub. The first fellow went in, leaving his two mates outside. He walked up to the bar, ordered a pint of bitter, drank it and started to walk away. 'Excuse me, sir,' said the barman. 'You haven't paid for your drink.'

'Of course I paid for it!' said the fellow, and walked out. The barman, who was new, thought he must have been mistaken, so he let it go.

The second fellow walked in and went through the same procedure. As he was about to leave, the barman said, 'How about paying for your drink, sir?'

'Are you joking?' said the second chap. 'I saw you put the money in the till!' – and out he walked.

Then it was the turn of the third fellow. He walked up to the bar and ordered his drink and the barman said, 'I must be going crazy! Two fellows have just walked in here, ordered a drink, then swore they'd paid – but I'm sure they hadn't! What's going on?'

'I don't know, I'm sure,' said the third customer as he finished his drink. 'But, look, I'm in a hurry, so just give me my change and let me get out of here, will you?'


*First Irish Drunk:* I heard a rumour that you were dead.
*Second Irish Drunk:* Yes, I heard that rumour myself, so I made a few enquiries and I found out that it was some other fellow entirely.

A customer walked into a pub and asked for a pint of beer and a large whisky. He drank the beer and then poured the whisky into the top pocket of his jacket. He ordered the same again, and once more he drank the beer and poured the whisky into the top pocket of his coat.

Several drinks later, the barman could restrain his curiosity no longer. 'What's the idea of pouring good whisky in your pocket like that?' he asked.

'None of your damn business!' snapped the drunk. 'Any more cheek from you, and I'll wipe the floor with you!' At that moment, a little mouse poked its head out of his coat pocket and snarled, 'And that goes for your damn cat too!'


'They say drinking shortens your life.'
'Rubbish! My grandfather drank a bottle of whisky a day and he lived to be ninety-seven. Mind you, they had to beat his liver to death with a stick!'


'If you try our Special Blended Japanese Whisky, we guarantee you won't wake up in the morning with a hangover! You'll get one right away!'


After a very heavy night of drinking, a fellow returned home from his club rather fearful of the tongue-lashing he would get from his wife. As it was six o'clock in the morning, he hit upon the bright idea of pretending that he had got up early to take a bath. He was splashing around merrily in the tub when his wife came in and said, 'What in the world are you doing?'

'What's it look like?' said the husband. 'I'm taking an early bath.'

'Well,' she replied, 'don't you think it would be a good idea to take your clothes off first?'

73

A drunk got on a train and sat opposite a Catholic priest. 'I shay, mister,' he said, 'you've got your collar on back to front!'

'I'm a Father,' said the priest.

'You don't shay! I've got two kids myself,' said the drunk. 'How many have you got?'

'I am the Father of hundreds,' said the priest with a smile.

'My God!' said the drunk. 'It's not your collar you should be wearing back to front – it's your trousers!'

A drunk was sitting in a bar when a customer walked in. 'Hello!' said the drunk. 'I haven't seen you for ages! Didn't you use to have a moustache?'

'I've never had a moustache,' said the customer.

'And you've lost a lot of weight,' said the drunk. 'And you've shrunk! You used to be six foot – now you're only about five foot six. And you look about twenty years younger. Anyway, it's nice to see you again, Maloney.'

'My name's not Maloney,' said the stranger. 'It's O'Connor.'

'Oh!' said the drunk. 'You've changed your name as well, have you?'

A drunk appeared at the ticket office at Victoria Station, with his companion slung over his shoulder. 'One adult and one child for Croydon,' he said.

'One child!' said the ticket clerk. 'Why that's a grown man – he's got a beard!'

'Dammit, Bert,' said the drunk, 'I told you to shave!'

He died from drinking beer
From an old tomato can.
So though the beer can't kill you,
An old tomato can!

The passenger on the London to Edinburgh train had obviously been spending a happy few hours in the buffet car. 'Offisher,' he said to the ticket collector, 'how far ish it from London to Edinburgh?'

'373 miles, sir,' said the ticket collector, and went on his way.

On his way back through the carriage half an hour later, he was again accosted by the drunk. 'How far ish it from Edinburgh to London?' he enquired.

'I just now told you how far it is from London to Edinburgh – 373 miles,' said the ticket collector. 'Obviously it's the same distance from Edinburgh to London!'

'Ish not obvious at all,' said the drunk. 'Ish jus' a week from Christmas to New Year, but ish a hell of a lot longer from New Year to Christmas!'

A prominent Tory politician frequently embarrassed his friends and colleagues by his addiction to the bottle. One day he went up north to make a speech in support of a prospective parliamentary candidate. His address to a large audience of Tory supporters was largely incoherent.

One of the reporters present, who rather liked the old boy, thought he would do him a favour by letting him see a transcript of the speech before publication. The politician made a large number of corrections and amendments to the transcript and sent it back to the reporter with the following note attached: 'Let me give you a piece of advice. Never attempt to take down a speech when you are as inebriated as you obviously were last night!'

A farmer returned home one night very much the worse for wear after spending the whole evening in the local pub. His hair and face were plastered with cow dung. 'What on earth's happened to you?' screamed his wife.

'Well, luv, I took a short cut across the cow pasture,' said the farmer unsteadily, 'and me cap blew off. I must have tried on a dozen before I found it.'

The friend of a notorious drunk had just become the father of twins. The drunk, who was in his usual befuddled state, went over to congratulate the parents. He gazed unsteadily down on the twins and then said cautiously, 'What a beautiful baby!'

The wonderful love of a beautiful maid –
The love of a staunch, true man –
The love of a baby unafraid –
Have existed since life began.
But the greatest love – the love of loves –
Even greater than that of a mother –
Is the passionate, tender and infinite love
Of one drunken bum for another.

After a heavy night on the tiles, Mike staggered into his flat, managed somehow to undress, and then collapsed into bed. He had no sooner dropped off than there was a knock on the door. Blearily, and with great difficulty, he stumbled out of bed and across the room. Opening the door, he found Joe standing there, his drinking companion of the evening. 'Did you take my umbrella by mistake?' said Joe. Then, noticing Mike's dishevelled state, he said, 'I'm sorry if I woke you up.'

'That's all right,' muttered Mike sleepily. 'I had to get up to answer the door anyway.'

A drunk on his way home staggered into a cemetery and fell asleep amongst the tombstones. Early next morning he was awakened by the sound of a nearby factory hooter. Rubbing his eyes, he sat up and muttered, 'Oh, my gosh, it's the Day of Judgement and I'm the first up!'

*First Cow:* You're not looking too well this morning.
*Second Cow:* No – I was up all night at a party and I've got a terrible hang-under.

'Would you like a drink?'
      'No, thanks.'
'Why not?'
'Well, in the first place, I am the secretary of the local Temperance Society. In the second place, today is the first anniversary of the death of my wife, and out of respect for her, I swore I'd never drink on this day. And in the third place, I've just had a drink.'

Three council workmen were sent to measure the height of the flagpole outside the town hall. They stopped off for a few jars on their way and were pretty tipsy when they arrived. They spent a couple of hours falling off ladders and trying to shin up the flagpole with a tape measure.

Eventually the borough surveyor came out of the town hall and explained that the flagpole could be unscrewed at the base and laid out across the municipal gardens. 'Is that so?' said one of the workmen sarcastically. 'Well, for your information, we were sent to measure the height of the pole – not the length!'

Did you hear about Jock and Sandy, two Scotsmen, who bought a bottle of whisky for £1.50? It was terrible — the worst whisky they'd ever tasted. They were halfway through it when Jock turned to Sandy and said, 'You know, I'll be glad when we've finished this!'

A drunk wandered into a cemetery whilst a funeral was in progress. He stood next to the vicar who was officiating at the ceremony and listened intently while the good man intoned, 'Ashes to ashes, dust to dust.'

Nodding wisely, the drunk looked round at the assembled mourners and said, 'Well, you can't say fairer than that!'

'How did you get on with your date last night?'

'We had a smashing time! I drank champagne out of her slipper!'

'What did it taste like?'

'Bollinger's — with a little bit of Dr Scholl's Corn Plaster thrown in.'

Magistrate: What evidence have you that the accused was drunk?

Policeman: Well, he walked up to the front door of a house, put 10p through the letter-box, picked up an empty milk bottle from the step, held it to his ear for a few moments, and then said, 'Damn it! No reply!'

Two Scotsmen were discussing the merits of Irish whiskey. 'Aye, I'll grant you it is useful stuff,' said one, 'If you run out of water for diluting your real whisky.'

Two drunks were weaving their unsteady way along London's Embankment late one Guy Fawkes' Night. A gang of skinheads had a roaring bonfire going at the foot of Cleopatra's Needle. The drunks stared at it for a few moments and then one said to the other, 'They'll never get it off the ground!'

A fellow who had been drinking all evening staggered over to the telephone at the back of the bar and dialled a number with some difficulty. 'Hello! Hello!' he shouted and a voice at the other end of the phone said 'Hello! Hello!' Banging the receiver down angrily, the drunk exclaimed, 'This phone has an echo!'

A drunk was sitting in a bar in an advanced state of intoxication. He turned to the fellow sitting next to him and said, 'Did you just spill your beer on my trousers?'

'No, I didn't,' he replied.

'It's just as I thought,' muttered the drunk. 'It's an inside job!'

'You'll just have to give up drinking or you'll lose your eyesight,' the doctor told the Scots patient.

'Ah, weel,' he replied, 'I think I've seen everything that's worth seeing.'


Did you hear the one about the two drunks who were imbibing in a bar? Suddenly one of them fell flat on his face. The other looked down at him and said, 'That's what I like about Sam – he always knows when to quit.'


A woman was walking down the street one morning when she noticed a small boy drinking from a bottle of whisky. She walked over to him and said sternly, 'Why aren't you in school at this time of the morning?'

'Why the hell should I be?' replied the boy. 'I'm only four years old!'


*First Drunk:* What time ish it?
*Second Drunk:* It's eightish.
*Third Drunk:* I make it nineish.
*First Drunk:* Tennish anyone?


A lady at a party asked a well-known wine connoisseur if drinking so many different wines ever gave him a hangover. 'No,' replied the expert. 'It's the indifferent ones that produce that result.'

The following advertisement is reputed to have appeared in *The Times*: ATTENTION SHIP-IN-BOTTLE MAKERS. I WILL ACCEPT FULL BOTTLES OF WHISKY, GIN, RUM OR BRANDY – ANY BRAND – AND RETURN THEM EMPTY READY FOR INSERTION OF SHIP. PROMPT, CONSCIENTIOUS WORK GUARANTEED. REPLY BOX 1000.

'Give me a martini,' said the fellow at the cocktail bar. 'Very dry – one part vermouth and nine parts gin.'

'Yes, sir,' said the barman. 'Would you like a slice of lemon in it?'

'No,' snapped the customer. 'When I want lemonade, I'll ask for it!'

*Doctor*: I would suggest that the best thing for you to do would be to give up drinking altogether.
*Patient*: What's the second best?

An inebriate wandering the streets late one night was stopped by a policeman. 'What are you up to?' said the bobby. 'I want an explanation and I want it quick.'

'Offisher,' said the drunk, 'if I had an explanation, I'd have gone home to my wife!'

Have you heard about the new game, Alcoholics Anonymous Russian Roulette? You sit in a circle and they pass round a tray with glasses of tomato juice on it – and one of them's a Bloody Mary.

Mrs McTavish: I hear your husband won a case of whisky in the Christmas draw last year.
Mrs McNab: Aye, he did that – but he was out of hospital by the beginning of February.

Two befuddled fellows were sitting in a bar when they noticed a young lady sitting on her own. 'Isn't that Hortense?' said one.
  'I don't think so,' said the other. 'She looks relaxed to me.'

Sign in a bar: THE FINEST MEDICAL BRAINS IN THE COUNTRY SAY THAT WHISKY CAN'T CURE THE COMMON COLD. NEITHER CAN THE FINEST MEDICAL BRAINS IN THE COUNTRY – SO DRINK UP!

A drunk at a football match was on his feet, waving his arms and shouting encouragement to the home team. 'Oi!' shouted a spectator a couple of rows back. 'Sit down in front!'
  'I can't,' said the drunk. 'I don't bend that way!'

83

The intoxicated hotel guest went up to the reception desk and said angrily, 'Why didn't you call me at seven o'clock this morning as I asked?'

'Because, sir,' said the receptionist politely, 'you didn't get to bed until nine thirty.'

A friend of mine drinks quite a lot. I wouldn't say he's an alcoholic but he's the only guy I know who wears sunglasses to protect his eyes from the glare of his nose.

A drunk was sitting at the bar vainly trying to spear the last olive in the bottle with the aid of a toothpick. After several attempts, his neighbour said, 'Here, let me do it!' He grabbed the bottle and speared the olive on his first try. 'You see,' he said. 'It's easy!'

'Oh, sure, sure,' said the drunk. 'After I got it so tired, it couldn't get away!'

CHAMPAGNE: the drink that makes you see double and feel single.

'How's your husband getting on in hospital, Mrs Jones?'
'I think he's getting better, Mrs Smith. Yesterday he was trying to blow the foam off his medicine.'

I know a chap whose doctor advised him to cut down on the amount of whisky he drinks. So he's started using larger ice cubes.

I wouldn't say my friend is a heavy drinker, but he's ruined his own health drinking to everybody else's.

'My wife has one very irritating habit. She stays up until two or three o'clock in the morning.'
'What is she doing all that time?'
'Waiting for me to come home.'

'What is it that makes you drink so much?'
'Nothing makes me, lady – I'm a volunteer.'

A noted evangelist was preaching to a rather hostile congregation. He asked if there were any questions and a voice from the back said, 'If you're as holy as you claim you are, can you walk on water?'
'Yes, my friend,' said the preacher. 'A great deal better than you can walk on whisky!'

The members of the Anti-Alcohol Society were always on the lookout for evidence of the advantages of total abstinence. Hearing of an old fellow of eighty-nine who had never touched a drop in his life, two of the committee members went round to his house to interview him. They hadn't been there more than five minutes when they heard a tremendous crash from the next room, followed by the sound of breaking glass. 'What on earth was that?' one of them asked.

'Oh, that's my father,' said the old man. 'He's probably drunk again.'

'I say,' said the drunk at the party, 'this is a very large gin and tonic you've given me!'

'That's the goldfish bowl!' said his host.

'Is it?' said the drunk. 'No wonder the slice of lemon keeps jumping up and smacking me in the face!'

# The World's Best Motoring Jokes

## Edward Phillips

It's generally agreed that the part of the car that causes the most accidents is the nut that holds the wheel . . .

| | |
|---|---|
| *Garage mechanic:* | *'The trouble is your battery, madam. It's flat.'* |
| *Lady driver:* | *'Oh dear! What shape should it be?'* |

| | |
|---|---|
| *Traffic policeman:* | *'Didn't you hear me shout to you to pull over?'* |
| *Motorist:* | *'I'm awfully sorry. I thought you said "Good morning, Chief Constable."'* |
| *Traffic policeman:* | *'That's all right, sir. I just wanted to warn you that the traffic's pretty bad up ahead.'* |

Whether you're a wheel-nut or a nervous passenger, a motoring maniac or just a back-seat driver, this collection of hilarious anecdotes and one-liners is an essential addition to every glove compartment.

0 00 638265 7

# Henry Beard and Christopher Cerf

# Sex and Dating

## The Official Politically Correct Guide

If you thought going on a date was simply a question of spending time with the opposite sex – think again! Dating is a consequence of 'phallocratic social conditioning', and before you indulge in such 'heterocentrism', or even 'consensual love-making', you must learn the language and the rules of the be-sensitive-or-else 1990s.

Only Henry Beard and Christopher Cerf can guide you through the politically correct minefield of sexual etiquette – what to do, where to do it, what to call it, who to do it with, and what they'll do to you if you try. Don't even think about calling your significant other until you've read this informative, hilarious and increasingly topical book.

Romance isn't dead, it's just 'terminally inconvenienced'!

0 00 638377 7

# The Official Politically Correct Dictionary and Handbook
## Henry Beard and Christopher Cerf

Welcome to the Nineties! But you'd better watch what you say . . .

Do you remember when people were 'dishonest' not 'ethically disorientated', 'drunk' not 'chemically inconvenienced,' 'fat' not 'horizontally challenged' or 'old' not 'experientially enhanced'?

You do? then you must forget such political incorrectnesses – and learn the language of the future. Only with this comprehensive, exhaustively researched reference work can you find out exactly what you can say, what you can't say, who says, and why.

Read this book and never again will you refer to: *the ugly bald shoplifter who is a sadomasochistic wino*. You will be politically correct and say: *the cosmetically different, follicularly challenged nontraditional shopper is a differently pleasured, substance abuse survivor!*

Whether you're oppressor or victim (or both) *The Official Politically Correct Dictionary and Handbook* is essential – and highly entertaining – reading.

ISBN  0 586 21726 6

# The World's Best Marriage Jokes

## Ernest Forbes

At last, the World's Best Jokesters turn their attention to the immortal subject of wedded bliss – or otherwise!

*A man got a gravestone for his wife while she was still alive. On it, he had the stonemason carve:*
  *'Here lies my wife, cold as usual.'*
*His wife was very angry so she had a gravestone for her husband carved with the inscription:*
  *'Here lies my husband, stiff at last.'*

*'What makes you think you've got a perfect husband?'*
*'Well, he remembers my birthday, but forgets my age.'*

*'I've just heard the strangest thing,' observed the husband to his wife. 'It seems our milkman claims he's slept with every woman in the street except one. Can you believe that?'*
  *'Oh, I believe it,' replied his wife sharply, her eyes glinting. 'I bet it's that stuck-up cow in number 4.'*

Whether you're a husband, wife or best man, whether you've taken the plunge or are just thinking about it – here's a book to entertain, educate, and give to your nearest and dearest!

ISBN 0 00 637839 0

# The World's Best After-Dinner Jokes

## Edward Phillips

The *crème de la crème* of the joke world, courtesy of the world's best jokesters.

Tall tales, naughty narratives and silly spoofs are all a part of that hitherto unacknowledged literary genre, the after-dinner joke. Gathered together in this new collection are the *World's Best* specimens of this much-practised but rarely excelled-at art form.

*A young lady was talking to an astronomer at a party. 'I can understand how you people work out how far the stars are from the earth, and what their sizes are,' she said, 'but how on earth do you find out what their names are?'*

*The old man was dying and he called his wife and family to his bedside. There were four sons – three fine big boys and a little one. He said to his wife in a weak voice, 'Don't lie to me now – I want to know the truth. The little one – is he really mine?'*

*'Oh, yes, dear,' said the wife. 'He really is, I give you my word of honour.' The old man smiled and slipped peacefully away. With a sigh of relief, the widow muttered, 'Thank God he didn't ask me about the other three!'*

The perfect accompaniment to any meal, *The World's Best After-Dinner Jokes* should go down very well indeed with the port and cheese.

ISBN  0 00 637960 5

## Please find listed below more humour titles available from HarperCollins:

| Title | Author | ISBN | Price |
|---|---|---|---|
| French For Cats | Henry Beard | 0 00 637823 4 | £4.99 |
| Advanced French for Exceptional Cats | Henry Beard | 0 00 638078 6 | £5.99 |
| Official Exceptions to the Rules of Golf | Henry Bead | 0 58621843 2 | £6.99 |
| The Official Politically Correct Dictionary | Henry Beard | 0 586 21726 6 | £4.99 |
| Girl Chasing | Cathy Hopkins | 0 00 637940 0 | £4.50 |
| Keeping It Up | Cathy Hopkins | 0 00 637855 2 | £4.99 |
| Merde! | Geneviève | 0 00 637793 9 | £5.99 |
| Merde Encore! | Geneviève | 0 00 637785 8 | £5.99 |
| Wicked French | Howard Tomb | 0 207 16665 X | £2.99 |
| Wicked Italian | Howard Tomb | 0 207 16666 8 | £2.99 |
| World's Best Business Jokes | Charles Alverson | 0 207 16385 5 | £2.99 |
| World's Best Drinking Jokes | Ernest Forbes | 0 207 16607 2 | £3.50 |
| World's Best Marriage Jokes | Ernest Forbes | 0 00 637839 0 | £3.50 |
| More Golf Jokes | Ernest Forbes | 0 00 637934 6 | £3.50 |
| World's Best Dirty Limericks | Harold H Hart | 0 207 14650 0 | £2.99 |
| World's Best Irish Jokes | Des Machale | 0 207 14836 8 | £2.99 |
| More World's Best Irish Jokes | Des Machale | 0 207 15069 9 | £2.99 |
| Still More of the World's Best Irish Jokes | Des Machale | 0 207 16880 6 | £2.99 |
| World's Best Scottish Jokes | Des Machale | 0 207 15805 3 | £2.99 |
| World's Best Golf Jokes | Robert McCune | 0 00 637802 1 | £2.99 |
| More of the World's Best Dirty Jokes | Mr J | 0 207 14231 9 | £2.99 |
| Still More of the World's Best Dirty Jokes | Mr J | 0 207 14730 2 | £2.99 |
| More World's Best Drinking Jokes | Edward Phillips | 0 00 637959 1 | £2.99 |